D0895612

NO LONGER PROPERTY OF
SEATTLE PUBLIC LIBRARY

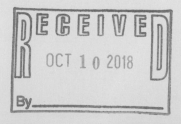

RECEIVED

OCT 1 0 2018

By

Rookie Poetry™

Holidays

let's celebrate

christmas

by J. Patrick Lewis

Children's Press®
An Imprint of Scholastic Inc.

Library of Congress Cataloging-in-Publication Data
A CIP catalog record for this book is available from the Library of Congress

No part of this publication may be reproduced in whole or in part, or stored in a retrieval system, or transmitted in any form or by any means, electronic, mechanical, photocopying, recording, or otherwise, without written permission of the publisher. For information regarding permission, write to Scholastic Inc., Attention: Permissions Department, 557 Broadway, New York, NY 10012.

Produced by Spooky Cheetah Press
Design by Anna Tunick Tabachnik (www.atunick.com)
Fonts: Coco Gothic, ITC Stone Informal
Clouds by freepik.com
Special thanks to Pamela Chanko for editorial advice

© 2018 by Scholastic Inc.
All rights reserved. Published in 2018 by Children's Press, an imprint of Scholastic Inc.

Printed in Heshan, China 62

SCHOLASTIC, CHILDREN'S PRESS, ROOKIE POETRY™, and associated logos are trademarks and/or registered trademarks of Scholastic Inc.

1 2 3 4 5 6 7 8 9 10 R 27 26 25 24 23 22 21 20 19 18

Photos ©: cover: Per Breiehagen/Getty Images; back cover: Per Breiehagen/Getty Images; 1: Per Breiehagen/Getty Images; 4-5: Per Breiehagen/Getty Images; 6-7 main: Per Breiehagen/Getty Images; 7 presents: Fuse/Getty Images; 8 sprinkles: Jan Lennart/Shutterstock; 9 gingerbread house: Claudia Paulussen/Dreamstime; 9 gingerbread man: eli_asenova/iStockphoto; 9 candy: Jim Esposito/Getty Images; 9 gingerbread ornaments: eli_asenova/iStockphoto; 9 candy canes: SAJE/Shutterstock; 9 gingerbread tree: CPaulussen/Getty Images; 11: Per Breiehagen/Getty Images; 12 nutcracker: Francesco Zerilli/Alamy Images; 12 stocking: Dorling Kindersley ltd/Alamy Images; 12 envelope: JGI/Jamie Grill/Media Bakery; 13 bottom left: Per Breiehagen/Getty Images; 13 center: Per Breiehagen/Getty Images; 13 right: JBryson/iStockphoto; 13 sign: Valeriya Zankovych/Shutterstock; 13 snowflakes: Simonas Šileika/Dreamstime; 14-15 garland: MattStauss/iStockphoto; 14 bottom right: Ermolaev Alexander/Shutterstock; 15 main: Jana Morozova/Shutterstock; 15 fireplace: Dmytro Grankin/Alamy Images; 15 wreath: marilyn barbone/Shutterstock; 15 bottom right: Africa Studio/Shutterstock; 15 nutcracker: Dan Kosmayer/Alamy Images; 15 left, center right stockings: Ozgur Coskun/Shutterstock; 15 center left stocking: LiliGraphie/Shutterstock; 15 center right: A-Basler/iStockphoto; 15 right stocking: Ozgur Coskun/Shutterstock; 16 top: Steve Collender/Shutterstock; 16 bottom right: Dan Kosmayer/Shutterstock; 17 background: azndc/iStockphoto; 17 center: Christopher Elwell/Shutterstock; 17 top center left: redstallion/iStockphoto; 17 top center right: Kord/Media Bakery; 17 top right: motorolka/Shutterstock; 17 top left: eli_asenova/iStockphoto; 18: nikolay100/Shutterstock; 19 main: ArtBoyMB/iStockphoto; 19 top sleigh: Per Breiehagen/Getty Images; 19 extra lights: Michael Wheatley/Getty Images; 20 top left: Ian Forsyth/Getty Images; 20 bottom right: Kucher Serhii/Shutterstock; 20 top right: Mirrorpix/Newscom; 20 bottom left: Kucher Serhii/Shutterstock; 21 bottom left: Silvia Izquierdo/AP Images; 21 top: Alex Coppel/Newspix/Getty Images; 21 bottom right: Reinhold Matay/AP Images; 22 bottom right: udra11/Shutterstock; 22 top, center: eli_asenova/iStockphoto; 23 top: thomaslenne/iStockphoto; 23 center top: esp_imaging/iStockphoto; 23 center: Phillip Minnis/Dreamstime; 23 center bottom: Jose Luis Pelaez/Media Bakery; 23 bottom: imanhakim/Shutterstock.

Scholastic Inc., 557 Broadway, New York, NY 10012

table of contents

merry christmas!

The snowman peeks through
  the window.
Christmas shows up everywhere.
The tree is a-sparkle with tinsel,
and sleigh bells ring
  through the air.

FACT!
In the U.S.,
9 out of 10
households
celebrate
Christmas.

all we want for christmas

The Squirrel wants a honey-roasted nut. The Fish wants chocolate sprinkles, but the Cat wants a frozen yogurt treat, and the Dog wants a leather shoe to eat!

FACT!
200 years **ago**,
people **used**
to put presents
on the tree—
not under it!

gingerbread house

Chocolate caramel gates and shutters,
frosted **spouts** and ribbon **gutters**.
Candy canes to build the fence,
deck the door with peppermints.
Cookie roof in place of shingles—
I know! This must be Kris Kringle's!

8

FACT!
The biggest-ever
gingerbread
house was
longer than a
school bus!

donner and blitzen

Two famous reindeer are thinking,
"We're getting ready to fly
'cause Santa's sleigh keeps on blinking,
which means let's fill the sky."

FACT!
A reindeer's nose warms cold air before it reaches the animal's lungs.

the secret helpers

Elf helpers and Mrs. S. Claus
deserve to be heard from because
they sit in the den
icing gingerbread men
while Santa gets all the applause.

FACT!
Every year, the
post office gets
millions of
kids' letters
for Santa.

NORTH
POLE

when santa prefers the door

He remembers
those Decembers,
burning **embers**, chimney holes
when he splendidly descended,
but rear-ended...on the coals!

FACT!
More than 700
million children
expect a visit
from Santa on
Christmas Eve.

sing a jolly song

Christmas carols—raise your voice!
'Round the living room, **rejoice**
at our sweet, long-needled tree.
Who will pass out presents? Me!
Who will keep the spirit bright?
Each of us by candlelight.

16

CHRISTMAS
CAROLS

FACT!
In 1906,
"O Holy Night"
was the first
song broadcast
on the radio.

the stars shine on

This house is a bright celebration
of Christmas lights, **holly**, and cheer.
The stars shine on these decorations—
I wish it stayed like this all year.

FACT!
Thomas Edison invented the first string of outdoor Christmas lights.

christmas around the world

Austria

Better be nice
Here, St. Nicholas travels with a giant horned monster called the Krampus. The Krampus punishes naughty children!

Kenya

Indonesia

Happy Cluck-mas
People on the island of Bali make special Christmas trees—from chicken feathers!

A bumpy ride
It is too hot in East Africa for reindeer. So when Santa visits Kenya, he travels by camel instead.

Argentina

Sparkly celebration
In Argentina (as in all lands south of the equator), Christmas falls in summer. Instead of building snowmen, people in many South American countries set off fireworks.

Australia

Hoppy holidays
Here, Santa borrows six white boomers to help him deliver gifts. (Boomer is a name for a male kangaroo.) People even sing a carol about them!

Bahamas

Dance party
People on this island wrap up Christmas with a colorful parade called Junkanoo. Musicians and costumed performers dance through the streets of Nassau.

21

christmas is...

...a holiday celebrated by millions of people around the world. It falls on the same day every year: December 25.

Christmas started out as a religious holiday. It is still celebrated mostly by Christians. Christmas celebrates the birth of Jesus.

There are many Christmas traditions for people to share. Some families attend Christmas Eve Mass together. Others celebrate with a big family meal. Many gather around the Christmas tree to exchange gifts. People also sing Christmas carols and decorate their homes with colorful lights.

Christmas is a time for peace and joy.

glossary

embers (EM-burz): The hot, glowing pieces of a fire after the flames are gone.

gutters (GHUT-urs): Shallow troughs or channels through which rain is carried away from the roof of a building.

holly (HAH-lee): A tree or bush with red berries and leaves with sharp points.

rejoice (ri-JOIS): Feel great joy or happiness.

spouts (SPOUTS): Pipes, tubes, or openings through which liquid flows or is poured.

index

facts for now

Visit this Scholastic Web site to learn more about Christmas:
www.factsfornow.scholastic.com Enter the keyword **Christmas**

about the author

J. Patrick Lewis has published 100 children's picture and poetry books to date with a wide variety of publishers. The Poetry Foundation named him the third U.S. Children's Poet Laureate.